PENGUIN BOOKS

THE SPIKE MILLIGAN LETTERS

Spike Milligan was born at Ahmednagar in India in 1919. He received his first education in a tent in the Hyderabad Sindh desert and graduated from there through a series of Roman Catholic schools in India and England to the Lewisham Poly-technic. Always something of a playboy, he then plunged into the world of Show Business, seduced by his first stage appearance, at the age of eight, in the nativity play of his Poona convent school. He began his career as a band musician, but has since become famous as a humorous script writer and actor in both films and broadcasting. He was one of the main figures in and behind the infamous Goon Show. Among the films he has appeared in are: *Suspect*, *Invasion*, *Postman's Knock* and *Milligan at Large*. Apart from *Puckoon*, Spike Milligan has also published *The Little Potboiler*, *Silly Verse for Kids*, *Dustbin of Milligan*, *A Book of Bits*, *The Bed-Sitting Room* (a play), *The Bald Twit Lion*, *A Book of Milliganimals*, his war trilogy, *Adolf Hitler: My Part in His Downfall*, '*Rommel: Gunner Who?*' and *Monty: His Part in My Victory*. Among his latest publications are *The Milligan Book of Records, Games, Cartoons and Commercials* (1975), *Dip the Puppy* (1975) and *William McGonagall: The Truth at Last* (with Jack Hobbs; 1976). He has four children and lives in London.

Norma Farnes, who selected the letters, has been Spike Milligan's manager for eleven years.

The
Spike Milligan
Letters

Edited by
NORMA FARNES

Penguin Books

Penguin Books Ltd, Harmondsworth, Middlesex, England
Penguin Books, 625 Madison Avenue, New York, New York 10022, U.S.A.
Penguin Books Australia Ltd, Ringwood, Victoria, Australia
Penguin Books Canada Ltd, 2801 John Street, Markham, Ontario, Canada L3R 1B4
Penguin Books (N.Z.) Ltd, 182–190 Wairau Road, Auckland 10, New Zealand

—

First published in Great Britain by M. & J. Hobbs, in association with Michael Joseph 1977
Published in Penguin Books 1979

—

Copyright © Norma Farnes, 1977
All rights reserved

—

Made and printed in Great Britain by
Richard Clay (The Chaucer Press) Ltd, Bungay, Suffolk
Set in Monophoto Baskerville

For Rita and Dennis Lascelles,
just two beautiful people

My favourite picture of Spike – by Snowdon

Foreword

I've always wished to be a man of letters. Well apparently this book does it for me. Unbeknown to me my manager, under my very nose (in a crouching position) has all these years been secretly compiling a book from my correspondence. I often wondered what she was doing in my office. She never did a stroke of work for me. All the time *I* have been working for *her*. Time and time again she would come into my office when I was concentrating on a TV show, or a book and she would say 'You must rest, relax, why not write a letter to The Times or someone?', anything to stop me working. I would do her bidding. On the basis of this she is about to become rich. However I forgive her, and I will be back in the office next Monday morning working for her as usual.

Spike Milligan

Contents

Introduction

The publishers asked me to do an introduction to this book, and I said 'Yes, O.K.' and didn't give it another thought until I sat down to do it. I thought it would be easy, but never having done anything like this before, I can tell you I'm not finding it so.

How do you start an introduction to a book that someone has *given* you? Yes given! To begin with, it's got to be very rare for someone to give away a book, and say 'Just do it – you can have it' – and that's how it was!

I have been with Spike Milligan for many years. People ask me 'What is he really like?', if I had a pound for every time that question has been put to me, I could retire and go and live in the South of France. Better still, if I could answer it I would be a genius.

I joined Spike on the 22nd August, 1966, but looking back it seems I've never worked anywhere else, and yet again, it seems no time at all. Eleven years have just flown by – being Spike Milligan's Manager is everything and anything except boring.

The very nature of him giving me this book to edit should go under the piece in this book called 'Spike at his Best'. I'll tell you how it happened.

I was going through a pretty bad patch – a divorce – Spike had been through it all, and knew the mental strain only too well. When he discovered I had to pay out money to stay in the flat I was living in – he was horrified. And, one morning, when all this was going on, he came into my office and said 'How are you off for bread? – badly, I'll bet – well I'll have to think of a way you can earn some extra', and walked out of the office.

I had a lot on my mind at the time, and completely forgot all about it. Until about three or four days later, Spike came into my office and said 'I've been thinking about your bread situation', and I said 'Don't bother, I'll get a night job', and he said 'Seriously, Norm, why don't you go through my files and collate some of my letters – ask the publisher if he is interested in putting them into a book. They might sell, and at least that will tide you over for a bit'.

And that's how it all started. Mind you, there was a condition. He didn't want to know anything about it, didn't want to be asked an opinion, didn't want to see the choice of letters, or be asked any questions at all (which you can imagine was difficult, making my own choice from thousands of letters he writes every year, to all and sundry). And the position it put me in. A truly magnanimous gesture on his part, and what if he didn't approve, because he still hasn't a clue of what is going into the book – what a position to be in? All he has ever said is 'Surprise me, and give me the first copy when it's ready'.

So the selection was mine, and I decided that it would be the sort of book that showed all the facets of Spike Milligan. It would have been easy to make this a funny book – funny letters from Spike to all his friends, but frankly I don't think Spike is a funny man, a funny writer – yes, but after eleven years with him, I know the man, and there's a lot more to Spike than him just being funny.

He genuinely cares – not about the human race in general, but about people, animals, trees, buildings, the environment – the whole Planet. And I think, and until he reads this he doesn't know because I've never told him, he cares too deeply and too much. When he learns of a cruelty to human beings or animals, he gets enraged, and then frustrated if he can't do anything about it immediately, and then, worst of all, depressed.

But that's Spike, that's part of the make-up of the man, he won't change – he can't change, and you accept the whole parcel of the man, or you don't accept him at all. Spike being witty all the time would drive me insane – in the office there's absolutely no chance of that because, as I said, I know the man, and basically would not have it any other way (mind you there are times, when I'm driven to desperation, I might not agree with what I have just written).

Alan Clare, a personal friend of Spike's, and one of the most lovable people one could ever wish to meet – once said to me 'Spike is two people, number one is the greatest guy you'll ever wish to meet, and number two, I avoid like the plague'. It's not far wrong. He's complex, but then he's a neurotic.

For example, no matter what the situation is at the office, and I mean by that any form of crisis – and we have at least four a day – the birds must be fed. That in itself needs an explanation. Spike has a small balcony at the back of his office, and every day he feeds the birds, and he has names for them all. I can understand the pigeons are quite tame, but he has tamed the sparrows that come there, and they literally eat out of his hands. His favourite sparrow is Fred, that's because Fred is always last to catch on that the food is there, so Spike waits to see he gets his fair share. His favourite pigeon is Hoppity, because he's got something wrong with his foot, and every day they come to his balcony and he carries on a conversation with them. I still remember, and this always sticks in my mind, Spike opening the windows one New Year's day, and saying 'Happy New Year Lads'. On the balcony Spike has window boxes, and towards the end of the summer, only last year, he kept two wasps alive for weeks, by putting a spoonful of jam inside a jar, turned on its side, so they could get to it.

Yet this same man can cause absolute chaos and tension because he can't get someone on the telephone at the precise moment when he wants to talk to them. Poor Cliff Morgan (another great friend of Spike's), no matter where in the world he happens to be, and Spike wants to speak to him, Tanis, Spike's right hand girl, has to find him, and get him on the phone, and I tell you, once, only a couple of years ago, Cliff was in Austria, somewhere up a mountain, and God knows how, Tanis tracked him down and they eventually spoke. Spike adores Cliff and, thank God Cliff adores Spike and better still understands him.

The phone bugs Spike more than anything else in the world. He really hates them, and his phone is 'off the hook', more times than it's on. But when he puts it back on, and wants to speak to someone, they have to be there; everything is immediate with Spike, and if he asks Tanis to get him, say Peter Sellers, and the answer comes back 'Peter is in Australia', Spike's usual come-back is 'Isn't Australia on the phone', and by the time Tanis has found out which city, which studio, which hotel, which number, Spike can turn round and say (and this is after an hour of trying to find the person and eventually getting them on the phone), 'I've done a hundred things since then, and now I've forgotten what I wanted to talk to them about'.

I remember Ian McNaughton (Producer of his television shows), ringing me in absolute fits of laughter. He had left the BBC and had gone free-lance, and was living in Germany. He had walked into a hotel in Tel Aviv, and the receptionist said to him 'Would you please ring Spike Milligan, it's urgent'. Well, he simply couldn't believe it, he had been, as he said, 'on the high seas for six days', and apart from one person in Germany, no one knew where he was – he, in fact, was working for Israeli Television. But Tanis, because she knows she has to, or her life is Hell, had found that person in Germany, and in turn found Ian, in Tel Aviv. Ian rang me, because he couldn't believe it, and said 'that old bugger will find you anywhere in the world'.

For many people Spike has charisma. I can tell by the sort of questions people ask me, and the things they say about him, a favourite is 'oh, he's a bit mad, isn't he?' Spike is one of the sanest people I have ever met, they confuse madness with neurosis. He's very mercurial, yes, he gets depressed, and people who don't suffer from depression have no idea what it's all about, they come in two categories; the 'why doesn't he pull himself together' brigade, or the people, who from fear of not understanding, pretend it's not happening, because they cannot actually *see* anything physically wrong. But 'mad' he certainly is not.

In the business world he's terrible – that's because he has no time for trivia – all he ever wants to know from me is, where, what time, how long will it take, what do I have to do? That's why basically we have a good working relationship. Way back in 1967, he once said to me, and I quote, 'I've made a decision – as from today, I'm not making anymore decisions', (at the time we were discussing some business deal), and I said 'O.K. I'll make the decisions, provided you stick by them'. And he put out his hand, we shook hands, and it's been like that ever since; hence, where, what time, etc. etc. And when we shook hands, I knew he meant it, because when I tell people in the business world that Spike and I do not have a contract between us, or a Service Agreement, nothing written down at all, they don't believe me, but it's true. When I joined Spike, he said to me: 'Let's see how it goes – we'll give each other a month,' and then he said 'Let's shake on it', and we did and the situation has never changed. That's how Spike likes to do business – he hates contracts, and sometimes when he comes into my office, and I'm reading a contract, he says 'Don't waste your time on all that, it's all shit', and he means it.

In this book I've tried to capture the many facets of Spike. Reading through it I'm not sure whether I've succeeded, but I think I may have achieved enough to give the reader an insight into his character.

NORMA FARNES

Acknowledgements

I would like to express my thanks to all the contributors in this book, who were all so helpful when I approached them about publishing their letters or photographs. Absolutely everyone was good enough to give their permission immediately.

A special thanks to Jack Hobbs (co-publisher), who was long suffering, and patient, mind you not all the time, and last but not least to Diana Holloway who constantly nagged me to 'get on with it', but for her I may never have got around to it.

At the Bayswater
Loony Bin

Slim Miller, who in 1972 was manager of The New Seekers, had an office in our building; when they moved we received hundreds of letters for them. After several phone calls to come and collect the mail, which they didn't, this is Spike's plea for help

22nd June, 1972

Dear Slim,

The inmates of my office are taking mountaineering lessons and using breathing apparatus every morning to surmount the South Col of the mountain called The New Seekers Height.

Samples of this mountain have been taken and analysed as being made from fan letters, some 2,000 years old.

Would you please collect the fucking things, it is cold up here.

Love, Light, and Peace,

SPIKE

A. I'm not in.   B. I'm very ill.   C. Don't let *ANYBODY GO IN MY ROOM* tell Tanis, Shona etc.   D. I've had enough – Jesus had it easy.   E. I'm at home.

Leave me
alive or there
would be a
bloody shin

My love is like a red, red rose—but my underwear is off-white.

Love from
Spike

Lo! a great star came in the Sky.. ..

To
Norma
from
Spike and Family

A Merry Xmas
1966
Pax in Terra

THE BULB IS MISSING FROM THIS ROOM.
I HAVE TAKEN IT OUT BECAUSE THE
LIGHT IS CONTINUOUSLY LEFT ON.
IT WAS LEFT ON ALL WEEK-END.
IF ANYBODY WANTS TO PUT A BULB IN
THEY MAY DO SO, BUT THIS MAKES
THEM RESPONSIBLE FOR THE LIGHT TO
BE SWITCHED OFF AT NIGHT.

SIGNED: *S. Milligan*

I will be responsible

Re Dentist Spike at his worst when I've already cancelled four appointments

Norma—
To hell with the
Dentist! Tell him
Sorry— or Hate me!
love
Spike

Spike, Peter Sellers, Bill Kerr, Alan Clare – Alan's birthday. I'm the one on the right

Spike Confused

Mrs Alistair MacLean sent Spike a telegram inviting him to a Christmas party – this was his reply, when he forgot the date

13th January, 1976

Dear Mrs MacLean,

I must apologise for not replying to your telegram but Christmas for me is like a blind man being thrown into a monkey pit to look for a hat pin and I may add strapped into a wheelchair with the wheels immobile.

I found your telegram today in my diary under 27th January and I was getting into my black tie as requested when I realised the party had been on 11th December. Do forgive me, everybody else has.

Happy New Year to you and Malcolm Livingstone.

Love, Light and Peace,

SPIKE MILLIGAN

9 METER BAY IN CAROLINE
PLACE EMPTY

ALL Meters
Booked. Residents
bays full —
I cant eat the
car

          Sprho Milkyas

My TV Set is
faulty — the
sound interferes
with the picture.
please mend when
I'm in MADRID
CYPRUS
AUSTRALIA

One of the usual kind of messages Spike leaves on my door

Norm— I come back at lunch. I don't know where you are.

The Fucking Grass

Norma –

13 July 5.30. I've just spoke
to Nanna – a boy from gentle
Ghost arrived yesterday – he
waked on the Lawn for 2.
hours – ~~then was~~ he
didn't finish the Job –
the edges need cutting with
shears — The ~~Rotor Scythe~~
~~Tota~~ He then asked Nanna
for £2. 50 – she paid –
This is getting to be a full time
job for me. WILL YOU GET SOMEBODY
ANY BODY TO FINISH THE
FUCKING JOB FROM START TO
FINISH — AND THEY DON'T
GET PAID UNTIL BOTH

LAWNS ARE CUT and
trimmed – and all grass
cuttings dumped in the
stream

PLEASE IF I
COME BACK AND
NOTHING HAS HAPPENED
Its the end
Love
8pel

The Joker with the Rotary
Sythe hasn't appeared

33

Whenever Spike needs anything from shops it's either:
'Out of stock'
'Out of print'
        or
'No we don't make those anymore'

and delightful Tanis who does all his shopping gets all his
instructions in great detail, as in the case of the morning
currant buns which should contain their fair quota of currants
but, according to Spike, never do, viz

After a silver disc, still skint

On one of those rare occasions when Spike opened the mail this was a typical comment and typical confusion

ACKNOWLEDGEMENT OF ORDER TO			№	5614

TELETRONICS LIMITED,

01-723 7443

FROM   Spike Milligan Productions LTD

FOR DELIVERY TO

QUANTITY	CAT. NO.	DESCRIPTION	
		Service call	
		Fault not known	
		Price to be advised	
		Which was ridiculous?	
		Now called to	
		Service my TV.	
		It was sent out	
		To Olympic Electronics	

DATE 14. / 1 / 70   per pro TELETRONICS LTD.

CUSTOMER'S REFERENCE Mr Milligan

6823-FL.   CA.

36

This was my reply together with another typical comment

MONDAY 19/1/70

THIS WAS THE
INTERCOM AND NOT
THE TELEVISION SET

Norman

Idiots call them firm

Telefunken

37

Spike's letters to the rest of the world are long,
comprehensive and detailed
But Spike's letters to me are usually condensed and to the
point

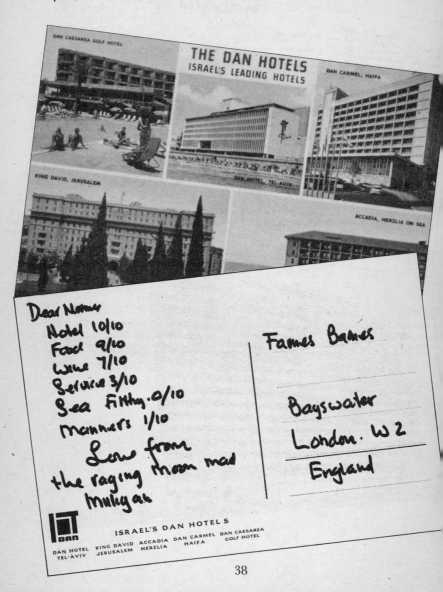

TEL AVIV HILTON

Situated in the heart of Tel Aviv, bounded on three sides by Independence Park, and on the other by the Mediterranean Sea. Entertainment and business area are within walking distance. All rooms and suites are air-conditioned and have panoramic view of the sea and the city.

P.S. The 'Med' is Brown

CURTEICHCOLOR® 3-D — NATURAL COLOR REPRODUCTION (REG. U.S.A. PAT. OFF.)

POST CARD

0.40

ישראל ISRAEL

Dear Miss Faines —
A Beautiful Picture
of ancient Israel.
The Yiddish Hilton (300BC)
excavated by an
American Capatalist.
Took 5 hrs to fly here
Love Spike

Naima Faines

Bayswater
London
W 2

39

TEL AVIV ⚡ HILTON

INDEPENDENCE PARK
TEL AVIV   ISRAEL
TELEPHONE: 24 42 22

Dear Norma.

Arrived after dark — its Raining.

Hotel very sprauncey — grub good —
Weather terrible. Got Pissed — home soon
Enclosed for Cliff Morgan Love to John
Tams. — and Eric Sykes Secretarias Legs.

Lou
Spk

MALTA G.C. —
—MOSTA CHURCH—
Designed by George Grognet de Vasse, it has
one of the largest unsupported domes in the
world.

Me dear tortured Contact ridden Jessie —
Weather super — sea clean — all the
family having tantrums — but I'm ok.
new moon — windy — good group at
Hotel bar — Beautiful Island. Food
70 per cent — wines OK. Hotel 8/10.
So far so good. Money arrived monday —
Spending like mad on the women
in the family. Jane is a joy to
be with — Swimming a lot — playing
tennis. I think you would like it here.
Love to all the birds + Tams
Lou   Spike

COPYRIGHT: THE CATHEDRAL LIBRARY, SLIEMA

The Farnes - Barnes

Bayswater
London W2.

England

40

To hell with ~~dates~~

Hotel Alvor Praia

PRAIA DOS TRÊS IRMÃOS
ALVOR
ALGARVE   PORTUGAL
TELEGRAMAS SALVOROTEL
TELEF. PORTIMÃO 1380

My dear Norma,

Arrived O.K. The hotel is unbelievable.
Its like an M.G.M. 1930s set for an Astair-Rogers
musical, with out the 'cheap' look. Its only 18 months
old, modern [but exquisite modern] and furnished with
antiques, and modern repros on a very high
standard. Its set in semi-arid Countryside
on the Atlantic — so, unlike the 'Med' its tidal,
and therefore much cleaner, the water temperature
is crisp, how can I say, well as the air temperature is 82°, [with cooling sea breeze] on entering
the sea, it feels cold, but it really isn't, so
swims are delightfully refreshing. There are
breakers when the tide is in coming, but goes
calm at rip and ebb tide. The colour of the
sea is a blue/grey, with a heat mist that
part obscures the horizon, and gives a feeling
of the sea going into eternity, in times
past the sea has pounded the cliffs — wearing
down the beach to its present level, but

41

2

leaving rocky seemingly indestructable
towering rocks, that now stand up on
the beach up to heights of a 100 feet.
In between these rocks the sea washes
round making insane patterns in foam-
spray and sand.

3

After Sunset, the use concealed lighting to ½ light the rocks - not too bright - allowing them to appear in an etheral mystic light. For free measure we have a half moon appearing at 8 o'clock - waning and dissappearing at about 11.30 Due to moisture in the evening atmosphere - the moon gradually turns orange as it dips behind a headland to the South west, so, the efect of amber lit rocks and moonlight ~~for~~ reflected from shore to horizon is a free gift, and all visible from our bed rooms [all air conditioned]. We arrived after at the hotel at 8.15 -. We were all pretty hot and sticky, we revived when we saw the fanstatic accomodation, we all perked up? The whole accomodation is interlinked by a large lounge the size of the studio at 009, with a glass wall looking onto the Atlantic - plus a balcony out side the glass wall.

We decide to have dinner in the Lounge.
We drank Two Bottles of Natives - had dinner -
watched Don Giovanni on T.V. then went
for a walk on beach. Bed. I awoke
at 11 o'clock. All the family had been
on the beach since dawn. I went
straight in the sea. Swam, jumped,
dived, and made a twit of my self doing
tricks for children. Up to the swimming
pool, swam in there for 20 - minutes -
Sun 10 minutes. Down to the beach
½ in sea again. Dead. Lunch - all
Salads and iced orange drink. I just realised
I haven't been on a holiday for 2
years, the one I had in Australia wasn't
really a holiday - I worked all the time.

I'm glad we all had dinner before
I left. X to Ginger - Tanis - Jill
          Love Light and Peace
         (but where do you find it Daddy?)
         xxxxx Spike xx

44

Old comrades on hard times

Comrades on better times

Spike and Conservation

To: Ms Daphne Charters,
Beauty Without Cruelty

Dear Ms Charters,

May I make a kindly suggestion to you. I notice when I receive
parcels of goods from Beauty Without Cruelty, what is well
intentioned packing, but in essence is overpackaging on a large
scale. For instance I ordered some Beau after shave – four bottles,
which are all in plastic unbreakable bottles, then they are wrapped
in a plastic resilience pack, then they are placed in a cardboard
box (a) with tissue paper on top, and then (b) a lot of plastic shock
absorbers.

I find this all excessive in terms of the run down of our planet,
forests are being depleted at an alarming rate for paper, and the
tissue paper looks very nice in the box, but it is not necessary,
likewise all the other things I have mentioned. So, in future, might
I suggest in the interests of us all that the packaging is less
extravagant. It would be an economic saving for a start, and also
help towards easing the use of the earth's products.

I do hope you take this in the spirit it is meant.

Again thank you for your service, and I shall give you my continued
support.

Love, light and peace,

SPIKE MILLIGAN

Spike had a reply from Ms Charters explaining that the amount of packaging used is based on past experiences, liquid substances having to receive special care as when their containers break, other items are usually spoilt etc . . .

29th June, 1976

Dear Ms Charters,

Thank you for your letter, I take your points, now here are mine:

I have taken one of the bottles of After Shave, and thrown it at the wall, I even jumped on it, and it didn't break. So, whereas you might like to pack other people's goods, as you suggest, I most certainly will take the responsibility for my after shave, being packed in a cardboard box and nothing else, and that way I will feel better, O.K.?

Love, to all,

Love, light and peace,

SPIKE MILLIGAN

Ms Lynette Donald wrote asking Spike if he would write a
letter so they could display it in connection with animal
welfare year

11th August, 1976

Dear Lynette,

First, good luck with your Animal Welfare Year show at the
Edinburgh Festival.

The cause for Animal Welfare is also the cause for Man's
enlightenment; nobody but nobody in this world can claim to be a
human being of any standing unless he has regard and *concern*, and
better still, positive reaction to the suffering that has been going
on to the animal world since the beginning of time. And, believe
it or not, there are more animals undergoing agonised experiments,
beatings, and treatments in this year than ever before in the history
of man, not even the Roman Games can reach the tally, of
something like 10 million animals killed a year in scientific
experiments, and that is putting the figure at the lowest possible
level. It's more likely to be 50 million; we won't go into how many
are slaughtered for us to eat, so dear friends, what you do might
appear to be very small in the light of the problem, but one thing
you can be sure of, it's as vital as life itself.

Love, light and peace,

SPIKE MILLGAN

2nd July, 1971

Dear Sir,

Several months ago, when they started to demolish the old County Hall in Pall Mall, I went through to see if anything worthwhile could be saved for the National Trust, for which Lord Antrim has given me authority to do.

Fronting the old building was an iron column with a bird bath on top. I contacted Mr Fred Hurley of Cluttons who said 'Don't worry, we will save the bird bath and have it repaired'. Through Cluttons I tried to get them to ask the architects of the new building to include it in the piazza which will front this building. Alas, Mr Hurley did none of these things and has since left Cluttons. I started the whole thing again with Mr Ralph Clutton, who seemed less positive than Mr Hurley and has finally, I believe, contacted you to find out what to do with it.

I can't go through all this ritual again as I am a very busy man, and I was only trying to do what a public spirited citizen would do to preserve some of England's past. As nobody even knew of the existence of this bird bath, including yourself, the Crown Agents, or Cluttons, although I drew attention to it, on the strength of that I would be grateful if you would give permission for the bird bath to be given to the National Trust to preserve and install in an appropriate building somewhere. Just say 'yes' or 'no'.

Respectfully,

SPIKE MILLIGAN

51

CROWN ESTATE COMMISSIONERS
CROWN ESTATE OFFICE, WHITEHALL, LONDON S.W.1
Telephone: 01-839 2211 Ext.
Please address any reply to the Secretary

Our reference: 20271/4
Your reference:

8th July, 1971

Dear Sir,

Thank you for your letter of 2nd
July. Although Cluttons informed us about
two weeks ago of your interest in the bird
bath in front of the old County Hall site,
we have not yet been able to decide its
disposal (it will not be destroyed in any
case). I am afraid therefore that I cannot
say "Yes" or "No" in reply to your question
whether it can be given to the National Trust,
but only "may be".

I will give you "Yes" or "No" however
within a few weeks.

Yours faithfully,

(J. S. Hogg)

16th July, 1971

Dear Mr Hogg

While you are making up your mind to say yes or no about the
bird bath, vandals have broken one side of it.

Respectfully,

SPIKE MILLIGAN

A Mr Hadwin wrote about decay in church buildings – this is Spike telling people how to do things

21st March, 1968

Dear Mr Hadwin,

You don't say whether you are a clergyman, vicar or a Roman Catholic priest, so I'm not sure how to address you.

It's sad about all this dry rot, death watch beetle, and the like in churches.

I have written in the papers about how to avoid this; it appears suddenly that Salisbury Cathedral needs £250,000, you will agree that this amount points out the amount of negligence in the first place.

What I am saying is a surveyor for a church might cost £500 a year, and it should be common sense to do this for the church.

Having told you that I am sending you an autographed book which you might like to auction for the church.

But do spread my enlightened words around to your clerical fellows.

Sincerely,

SPIKE MILLIGAN

11th December, 1968

Dear Anthony,

I was delighted to read in the Sun, December 10, that you are
taking steps to prevent wilful neglect of old buildings (sometimes
important) allowing them to get into a condition that they are
condemned as unfit for human habitation, and then, of course,
selling the land and building flats at a great profit.

I wrote a long time ago to Richard Crossman saying that this was
one of the major destroyers of British architecture, which had it
been maintained in good condition would not only be habitable,
but also a joy to look at.

Congratulations on doing something about it at last.

Alas, in Finchley the last beautiful building, called Brent Lodge,
which I fought desperately to save had been let go by none other
than the Local Council themselves, and when I pointed out the
merit of the building, and an estimate of £20,000 would put it in
good order, their immediate reaction was to have the building
pulled down.

If your idea goes through this, of course, will stop these 20th
century vandals (and have no two ways about it I have never met
a Local Council with an aesthetic outlook) from pulling down the
last vestiges of buildings with some semblance of beauty.

Regards as ever,

SPIKE MILLIGAN

P.S. No need to reply to this letter, I know you are busy; if not
you should be.

To: M. H. Rubin, Esq.,
Editor,
The Progressive   14th May, 1970

Dear Mr Rubin,

Your magazine appears to have got out of America despite the
smog. It was a pleasant surprise to see it land on my desk. I don't
know for what reason you singled me out, but you might be pleased
to know that I am a conservationist, I belong to the World
Wildlife Fund and the Family Planning International, and
conservation groups throughout Great Britain.

Anyhow, thank you for the magazine. I was delighted to see that
Henry Gibson is a conservationist. Surprising that the lead towards
restoring the world's natural balance seems to be coming from
people like clowns, comics, actors, students, but very little from the
Pentagon or the White House. The world is changing, but I think
it needs a change at the top more than anywhere else.

Love, Light and Peace,

SPIKE MILLIGAN

*Spike – me – his mother
on his 58th birthday – Australia*

"Issue" (Furtherwick Park
School Newspaper)
32 Urmond Road,
Canvey Island,
Essex,
30. 12. 71.

Dear Mr Milligan,

Knowing of your active interest in the world wide problem of pollution of the land, sea, and air, we would be most grateful if you could write a few lines to us expressing your views on the subject. We hope that you can oblige us.

Yours Sincerely,
Jack Hoy and S. Mitchell
(editors of "issue").

56

To: Messrs. Jack Hoy & S. Mitchell,
Issue,
(Furtherwick Park School Newspaper)   *10th January, 1972*

Dear Lads,

Basically, here is the dilemma:

COPULATION EQUALS POPULATION
EQUALS POLLUTION.

ANSWER: BIRTH CONTROL.

Sincerely,

SPIKE MILLIGAN

To: The Chairman,
Messrs. Hardwicke,
Dublin   *19th May, 1971*

Dear Sir,

Might I put into writing my protestations against your
development in Molesworth Street. At the moment Dublin is the
last truly Georgian city left in the world and, looked at
economically, could become one of the greatest tourist attractions
in Europe if it survives. Most certainly people won't go to see
Dublin for mere functional buildings.

If you are an Irishman, and more so, if you are an Irishman with
feelings, I am asking you to consider the future of Molesworth
Street in this light. If you have no feelings then of course my letter
is wasted. If at some date I walk down Molesworth Street and see
the product of your company staring me in the face I will know
that you have no feelings, and for this I am very sad for you and
Dublin.

Respectfully,

SPIKE MILLIGAN

An ordinary circular letter arrived from Rank Xerox, offering equipment

Rank Xerox (UK) Limited
Northdale House
Abbeydale Road
North Circular Road
London NW10
Telephone 01 965 0051

RANK XEROX

5th April, 1973.

Dear Sir,

From the age of Leonardo da Vinci onwards men like Chester Carlson
have appeared once in every century or so to transform entire
technologies with a single invention.

As you'll see from the enclosed folder, Carlson's original Xerographic
principle has now developed into a comprehensive range of Rank Xerox
copiers and duplicators.

Even if you are already a Rank Xerox user, you'll find it well worth
while to get completely up to date on some of our latest machines like
the 7000 reduction-duplicator. Using this machine, you can print and
reduce simultaneously at a rate of 60 copies a minute. You can reduce
A3 originals for inclusion in a standard A4 size report or reproduce two
A4 size sheets side by side onto one A4 size copy. However you use it,
you effect a significant cost saving.

For the full story - and your free Leonardo reproduction print - simply
post the card attached to the folder. We'll show you our latest
inventions.

Yours faithfully,

MARTIN FORBES

Regional Managing Director
H.Orr-Ewing

Directors:
A. Bordone It., B.H.Nicholson, R.C.O'Donoghue
R.M.Pippitt USA, J.M.Thomas, J.S.Thomas

Registered Office: Bridge House, Oxford Road, Uxbridge, Middlesex
Place of Registration: England
Registered No. Rank Xerox (UK) Ltd: 330754

The following is his reply

To: *Martin Forbes Esq.,*
Rank Xerox (UK) Limited   *6th April, 1973*

Dear Sir,

Reference your circular of 5th April, as long as Rank insist on
pulling down the Gaumont at Notting Hill Gate, I have no wish
to do business with them.

Yours faithfully,

SPIKE MILLIGAN

Me – Marty – Spike
'they're beginning to look their age'
on location in Hollywood

Spike's campaigns don't stop at England. As soon as we arrived in Cyprus for a film – he's at it again

To: The Editor,
Sketch Magazine,
Beirut,
Lebanon   *15th October, 1973*

Dear Sir,

I recently arrived in Cyprus to make a film, and during the filming I was contacted by a Dr Dimitri Souliotis, regarding Mount Pentadaktylos, which he rightfully claimed is being mined and speculators possibly building houses all over it.

In the light of your article of 16th March, 1973 I can only support this man's diligent attempt to save this particular mountain from being degraded and ultimately destroyed by the heavy lack-lustre mind of money-making humans to the extent of de-beautifying their own environment.

One of the reasons this film is being shot in Cyprus was because of the attractive back-cloth that Mount Pentadaktylos afforded for this film.

If the Cyprus Government have any feelings of respect for the environment, they would purchase this mountain and leave it, that their children may see the sun strike it at dawn with that electrifying beauty that only nature can give to an appreciative civilised human soul.

The publication of this letter in your enlightening magazine would be a step forward in the right direction.

Yours faithfully,

SPIKE MILLIGAN
President Finchley Society,
Committee Member World Wildlife Fund

Spike had made friends with a Father Patrick Fury. They
had corresponded quite frequently, until this letter

28th March, 1975

Dear Father,

Just a brief note to ask how you are and whether the post-operative
condition is satisfactory.

I did enjoy my stay in Rhodesia, and of course that miraculous
quality called sunshine was everywhere, but never in the shade.

I saw a wonderful panorama of wild beasts and I, deep down, was
hoping that in 200 years time all these creatures may still exist, but
somehow I have my doubts. How can world population explode as
it is, and still leave room for animals?

One day, dear Patrick, when the Vatican is filled with the beds of
overflowing families our dear Pope might shout out enough is
enough, and at communion, not only give out the Host, but also
the pill, it would be a perfect combination, spiritual and physical
salvation. So spread the word dear Patrick.

Love, light and peace,

SPIKE MILLIGAN

Unfortunately Father Patrick Fury did not see eye to eye with
Spike – and wrote and told him the friendship must end

Spike Milligan is the President of the Animals' Vigilantes. He made a remark on radio's 'World at One', re the shooting of cats. He had a letter from Animals' Vigilantes saying a number of their supporters had resigned because of his statement. He also had a letter from the Three Counties Cat Society. This is his explanation

To: Ted Cox, Esq.,
Animals' Vigilantes

18th June, 1974

Dear Ted,

This letter will be a letter which you can photostat or copy and send to all those people who are 'outraged by my cruelty towards cats'.

It is very interesting that nobody seems at all concerned about the boy I shot, everybody said 'good, you should have shot him' but shoot a cat and the world is up in arms.

Now then, I am a man who is concerned with the whole spectrum of life and the sanctity of it, believe it or not last month, I was outraged at the treatment given to an earthworm on the Open University Programme and as a result of it, I wrote to Sir Charles Curran and the R.S.P.C.A. In the same week I was presenting a petition for the conservation of the largest living creature on earth, the whale, to the Japanese and Russian Embassies. So, no matter what these people think or say as the result of a report in a newspaper, they cannot take away from me the fact that I work on a greater scale of conservation than most of the people who are concerned with the pussy cats alone.

I have always been highly suspect of people who have only a one animal interest, these are usually the 'Pussy Cat people', or the 'Poor little doggie people', and in the main I find they are psychologically unbalanced, and have very little concern for any other living creatures, except the ones *they* worship and rather like those people who belong to the R.S.P.C.A. and hunt stags and foxes to death.

I notice that the Three Countries Cat Society are outraged by the fact that I keep an airgun to shoot at cats who come into the garden to hunt birds.

First, let me tell you that I have two cats of my own, both of whom I love and they love me, and are well fed and are well treated, we also have a rabbit, a guinea pig and a goldfish. I myself put up lots of nesting boxes in my garden; now, when I see a well fed sleek cat about to kill fledglings or raid the nests and I am unable to get there physically to stop their death I would take the action of shooting at the cat with an air pellet. This does no more than sting the cat and it saves the lives of helpless fledglings.

This act of mine is considered cruel, apparently I should stand by and let the cat destroy the fledglings and then the pussy cat people would be perfectly happy – well I'm afraid I cannot reduce myself to that minuscule method of thinking. They say the cats are natural predators, and although regrettable to bird lovers must be accepted as a natural function. Well if they believe in the cat's natural instinct, likewise I have the right to exercise mine, in this case to protect the fledglings.

To date I have never shot a cat as I have managed to shoo them away before they have destroyed the birds, but it's on the cards that if I can't get to the cat in time I will use the air rifle, which will save the lives of birds, and will do no more than sting the cat.

In conclusion, if people are going to sit in judgement of other people by what they read in newspapers, there is no hope for any of us.

I hope this letter has made clear my feelings and if the Animals' Vigilantes decide as a result of this letter that I am not a fit person to be the President, I am perfectly willing to resign. But,

63

nevertheless, I will still go on doing what I believe to be right because that is all I ever can do.

I would like to add that I am also a vegetarian as a protest against the outrageous factory farming, and likewise I do not use products made of leather, and I make sure that the cat food my cats eat is not from animals under threat of extinction like kangaroo meat. I wonder if any of the pussy cat people are doing as much.

As ever,

SPIKE MILLIGAN

The Affair of
the Antique Phones

Sir,

COPENHAGEN TELEPHONES

Recently I had the decor of my office changed to suit the period of the building, which is Edwardian. To match the decor I have bought three renovated antique telephones.

Can you tell me what I do about having my GPO telephones removed? Do I have to go on paying rental for GPO telephones that I am not using?

I would, of course, like them taken away, and the rental cancelled. Can you tell me what the laws are on this, and by that I mean statutory laws?

I do hope you can help me.

Respectfully,

SPIKE MILLIGAN

Telecommunications
Headquarters
Headquarters Building
St. Martin's-le-Grand
LONDON EC1

Telephone:
01-432 1234   (switchboard)
01-432 5790   (direct line)
Telex: 21166 (POHQ LDN)
Telegrams: Gentel London EC1

In any reply please quote: **28839/63**
Your reference:

28th May, 1968

Dear Mr. Milligan,

    Thank you for your letter of 20th May to the
Postmaster General about the connection of 'antique'
telephones.   I have been asked to reply.

    You may remember that back in 1963 you asked to
connect a German telephone to your switchboard.   We
had to turn down the request in accordance with our
policy, and our policy remains the same with regard
to non-standard telephones.   I am sorry, but your
Edwardian telephones must be disconnected although
it might be that you will have to redecorate your
office to suit our telephone instruments!

    A telephone instrument must be designed to work
with the GPO telephone system and is an important
link in the chain which includes intricate switching,
transmission and signalling equipment.   Therefore we
insist that all telephones used on the public exchange
network should be provided by the Post Office.

    As far as we are able we inform firms and stores
who are selling non-standard telephones of the restriction
on their use and ask them to let their customers know.

/Unfortunately

Unfortunately, it is not until a case such as yours
arises that we know they have not heeded our advice.

Since you have enquired about our statutory laws,
I am able to refer to them without you thinking me
heavy handed.   Telephone service and rentals are
covered by the Telephone Regulations 1965 which forbids
the connexion of unapproved apparatus to the public
network.   The penalty for contravention of these
regulations is a dire one, summary termination of
telephone service.

What enjoyment?

I am afraid that, if you wish to continue
enjoyment of the telephone service, the GPO telephones
must be reinstated in their proper place.   We will
make arrangements for a Post Office engineer to visit
your office to undo the work done ~~by the Fortnum
and Masons engineer~~ at a time convenient to yourself.

I realise how unkind it must seem to you on
having bought what must be handsome looking telephones
only to find that our Regulations prohibit it being
used on a public exchange.   Nevertheless, we believe
our policy to be best for our customers as a whole.

Yours sincerely,

S. A. Hewitt

(MISS S. A. HEWITT)

*Letter to: M Foot any M.P -
This is a negation of personal
choice - and freedom.*

68

5th June, 1968

Dear Miss Hewitt,

Thank you for your letter which confirms that dictatorship exists in our lives. I find it becoming increasingly unbearable to accept England as a democracy.

We are all gradually being seduced from freedom by laws.

You realise that when citizens in a country are tied down at every level by unending laws, it is just an inversion of Communism and Fascism.

You are (the GPO), in fact, telling me what kind of furniture I should have in my office.

If you don't find this outrageous, then obviously you have been thoroughly indoctrinated into the system.

There is no need to send your engineers because the antique phones have *not* been connected.

However, I intend personally to get the law changed. Somebody has got to fight against this monstrous thing called State.

I am throwing in my lot with the students.

Respectfully,

SPIKE MILLIGAN

Spike and the GPO

To: The Rt Hon Roy Mason, MP
Postmaster General   *27th May, 1968*

Dear Roy Mason,

In the building I now occupy there are numerous telephone lines
which have been installed over the past 30 or 40 years, which
have been disconnected, and consequently there is a stack of lines
around through the building. Can you send a person who will
verify what lines are being used, and take away the lines which
are now not in use.

The reason being they present an eye sore and a great spaghetti of
lines are around, over doors etc.

Will you treat this matter as urgent, I will tell you why, the last
GPO man in here said he would send someone along to do this,
needless to say he hasn't.

Sincerely,

SPIKE MILLIGAN

2

Several GPO engineers came – nothing happened – then on
27th November Spike received a letter saying it seems some
confusion exists over the telephone system, and Mr S. Marsden
the Sales Superintendent would make an appointment and
come himself

29th November, 1968

Dear Mr Marsden,

My secretary will make an appointment with you.

Briefly, the job I have been trying to get done for about six months is to remove from inside and outside of the entire building, all GPO telephone lines that are not in use.

Believe me, I have explained this to various GPO officials who have visited here to take down notes, but there still remain a lot of GPO cables, looking rather like spaghetti. I am only trying to make the building efficient and also to make the place look tidy.

Unfortunately, over the last fifty years there has been no restricting hand on any electrical or telephone engineers coming in and taking things up the walls, over the ceilings, and around the doorways and such like. That is the job I have been trying to get done.

The second part of my job is I want all lines attached to the back of the telephone switchboard that are not connected to any other lines in the building removed throughout the entire building inside and outside.

These are the two specific jobs I need doing, the third job is, of course, to remove all telephones that are not in use, including all lines that are attached to any junction boxes.

Briefly, a resume, all I want, inside and outside of the building are the wires removed which are not in use.

Sincerely,

SPIKE MILLIGAN

3

Mr Marsden then came and supervised some work on the building. When Mr Marsden took over things got going (he was a divine man), but on 2nd December Spike received a letter from the Deputy Telephone Manager to say he thought all the mess had been cleared up last May

4

To: A. D. Larrett Esq.,
GPO,
Centre Telephone Area

4th December, 1968

Dear Mr Larrett,

Without trying to sound rude, you don't appear to know what you are talking about, so there is no point in answering your letter.

I am now working with a Mr S. Marsden to whom I have written a detailed explanation and who is going to meet me here on site.

I assure you I commenced last May asking the GPO to remove all their surplus lines, and on that occasion a man came and took *some* away. Since then I have managed to get more and more lines removed by the GPO all of which have belonged to the GPO.

There are still wires hanging outside of the building which belong to the GPO.

Respectfully,

SPIKE MILLIGAN

5

Some further work was done

7th January, 1969

Dear Mr Marsden,

You remember you and your friends came round before Christmas and said you would be removing the surplus lines on the ground floor back office.

I have heard nothing since and I cannot hold up the decorators much longer. I wonder if you could tell me when they will be coming as it is now urgent.

Yours sincerely,

SPIKE MILLIGAN

6

Mr Marsden then came himself, and everything was cleared

19th February, 1969

Dear Mr Marsden,

Here we go again. I would like you to come again and please ask to see me. There has been some damage done by the GPO. They have broken the top lintel on a door and I would just like you to see it. When they took the cable off the top of the door they have obviously ripped it off. I assure you that this damage has been done by the GPO.

Sorry it has gone on so long but honestly it's not my making, it's the GPO's.

Sincerely,

SPIKE MILLIGAN

To: Telephone Manager's Office,
London North Telephone Area   *10th June, 1969*

Dear Sir,

Will you please ensure that all bills for my home telephone are
sent to Spike Milligan's office address and not, *repeat not* to Holden
Road, N.12.

The reason being anything delivered there is taken apart by my
four children, a dog and a cat and the cleaner.

Sincerely,

SPIKE MILLIGAN

To: London North Telephone Area   *17th July, 1969*

Dear Sir,

Can you tell me why I received a reminder for my telephone bill?
Was I behind with my payment? If so, how far behind?

Yours sincerely,

SPIKE MILLIGAN

Spike received a reply from North Telephone Area which said
that they had in fact received payment to clear the current
bill, but unfortunately the reminder was sent from the
computer before they had time to advise the computer of
his payment.

He replied

To: H. S. Wiramanaden Esq.,
North Telephone Area   5th August, 1969

Dear Sir,

Your letter of the 38th July, 1969 must have been a slip of the pen.

What you say in your letter is that because of the computer we have had to write to each other five times, which seems to make absolute nonsense of the computer, which is supposed to save a lot of trouble.

                                                    Yours faithfully,

4

To: Mr J. Stonehouse,
GPO   23rd June, 1969

Dear Sir,

For four months now I have found it impossible to get through from my office to my home. I have had two sets of engineers with screw drivers who have done things to the office number but the problem still remains. As a layman, let me tell you I think the following is a problem:

1) After six o'clock I believe the GPO throw the switch to night service for cheap calls, I think perhaps the mistake might be at any exchange.

2) The switchboard at my office might be faulty when it is set for the night; that or the phone at my home after six o'clock at night.

Could you get somebody to investigate this problem thoroughly, but don't send any more little men with screw drivers.

                                                    Yours respectfully,

5

Spike received a reply from Central Telephone Area on 14th July, 1969, saying that the difficulty was caused by faults on exchange equipment and all should now be well. However, all was not well and Spike instructed Tanis to tell them so. They replied on the 11th August, 1969, saying that they were going to make another series of tests

To: D. S. McCrone,
Service Superintendent
Central Telephone Area London   *13th August, 1969*

Dear Mr McCrone,

Your letter of the 11th August, reference CT/C/T1. Once again, I report that on the 12th August at 23.30 hours three calls from my office to my home failed to get through. I dialled the 727 exchange, who had to get through to the HIL exchange to verify no tone on my home number.

So, back to you chum.

Yours sincerely,

6

On 19th August, 1969, the GPO again apologised that Spike was still having difficulty and ordered a full investigation

19th August, 1969

Dear Mr McCrone,

Carrying on the story. On Sunday 17th August, 1969, two calls to my home didn't get through to the 727 operator. So, it's still as it was.

Love to have it fixed permanently.

Yours sincerely,

7

The G P O replied on the 15th September, 1969, about the continued difficulties and ordered further extensive tests which led to more faults being traced and put right. However

To: D. S. McCrone   *27th October, 1969*

Dear Sir,

The following is the continuing story of office calling home. The failures continue, but always after 6 o'clock at night; that is when my telephone is put through for the night, on the office switchboard.

Following failures:

    18th September ....1.00 pm
                                 8.00 pm (twice)
    23rd September ....11.00 am
                                 2.00 pm
    28th September ....6.30 pm (twice)
    2nd October ....7.00 pm
    8th October ....7.00 pm
    18th October ....3.30 pm
    11th October ....1.00 pm
    14th October ....6.30 pm

                            Yours sincerely,

                            SPIKE MILLIGAN

8

This resulted finally in a cure!

28th September, 1971

Dear Christopher,

The continuing story of my telephone. Sometime, whilst I was
away from my home during the last two weeks, a GPO man,
without any pre-warning, arrives at the house, takes the phone
away and puts another one in. I did not ask for this, nor to my
knowledge was there anything wrong with the phone; but the
previous phone I had, had the bells removed because, one, being
so close to my bed they were not necessary, and two, they gave me
a terrible shock.

The new phone now has the bells back in, I have taken the bells
out myself, but I don't know how to put the phone cover back on,
can the Johnny who came along and made a mess of it, please
come back and put the phone together again WITHOUT
THE BELLS.

Will they also please have the courtesy when they are coming to
phone and make an appointment with me, or my wife, or the
housekeeper, or my daughter or the gardener.

Once again the telephone is not usable because you cannot rest
the handset on the cut off switch, so I am still not paying for it.

Sincerely,

SPIKE MILLIGAN

To: A. W. C. Ryland Esq. CB.
Central Headquarters,
Post Office

8th March, 1972

Dear Sir,

I think attention should be drawn to the terrible state of franking of letters.

It's now almost only one in 20 that is legible, as to what date and time and place it was franked. If you want evidence I am willing to save the next 100 letters and send them to you.

I think a general directive to all Departments might improve the quality of this simple task.

I write this letter to you as a citizen concerned with improving our amenities.

Sincerely,

SPIKE MILLIGAN

An acknowledgement was received!

Trying to get his point over

Spike and the BBC

To: Sir Charles Curran,
British Broadcasting Corporation

21st May, 1975

Dear Sir Charles,

The B.B.C. programme Let's Join In, want to do a fairy tale of
mine, and in it they want to excise the word God, they say its
'policy principle does not allow the mingling of fact and fiction.'
Anyhow, I cannot contribute to such stupidity, and I am writing
to let you know the B.B.C. Departmental laws, and I have refused
to allow the word God to be cut out. The attached letter is self-
explanatory.

I am writing to you because I thought you might change this silly
rule.

Hope you are well Charles, and all goes well with you and your
wife.

Love, light and peace,

SPIKE MILLIGAN

01-580 4468
Broadcasts London Telex
Telex 22182

BROADCASTING HOUSE

LONDON WIA IAA

5th June 1975

Dear Spike,

Thank you for your letter of 21st May, earlier
acknowledged by my secretary. "Let's Join In" is a
Schools programme intended for infants and the producer
wanted to avoid conveying the impression to them that
God existed on the same level of reality as goblins,
witches and giants.   Neither you nor I believe that.
There is no policy against mingling fact and fiction,
only in this instance a wish not to confirm some
children's belief that God and His powers belonged to
the world of magic. As a believer, I think you will
recognise that there is a serious point here, and I do
hope you will reconsider your decision not to allow the
broadcast to take place.

Yours ever

Charles.

(Charles Curran)
Director-General

Spike Milligan, Esq.,

To: Sir Charles Curran

9th June, 1975

Thank you for your letter – you are a good man to take time to write letters, they are so important in giving one an insight of the writer.

Part 2. God versus Goblins.

My dear Charles,

I believe in Goblins *and* God; I think the combination is absolutely marvellous, of course, I like to get it very clear that all my Goblins are Roman Catholics, that's why when you go into confession, if you look on the floor you will find a long thin ladder leading up to the confessional window.

I refuse to give in Charles, but I am sure God will forgive you for not believing in Goblins.

I must go now, there is a fairy tapping on my window pane – wait a minute I think it's a Protestant, so I won't open it.

Love, light and peace,

SPIKE MILLIGAN.

P.S. I will give in, but only because you are all so unenlightened, I will allow the word God to be stricken from the record, but don't forget Charles, on the Great Day, when God says 'who told you to remove my name from that story?', you know who I will be pointing at.

01-580 4468
Broadcasts London Telex
Telex 265781

BROADCASTING HOUSE

LONDON W1A 1AA

10th June 1975

Dear Spike,

Thank you for your covering letter of 9th June, which is nice about me. Why am I not nice to Goblins - or, at least, not as nice as you are?

Well, simply because I am a Director-General, which means that I am only allowed to believe in things that other people tell me. Of course, as me - Charles Curran - I am perfectly free to believe in Goblins, even in the Confessional. And like you, I am quite sure that they are all Roman Catholics, and that when we come out of the Confessional they carry away our sins in little bags and put them in the collecting boxes, where, of course, they turn into buttons! (You always knew, didn't you, that it was not little boys who put buttons in the box?)

And if God asks me on the great day, "Why did you take my name out of that story?" - I shall say, "Not me! Blame the BBC - like everybody else does!"

And thank you for being so generous about allowing God to be invisible in your story. He really is, you know!

Yours ever
Charles

(Charles Curran)
Director-General

Spike Milligan, Esq.,

87

Your humble servant Ma'am

The Bupa Affair

4th May 1971

Dear Sirs,

I recently had a full medical check-up at your BUPA Medical Centre and they asked on a pamphlet had I any suggestions.

1. I think the gruesome short dressing gowns the men have to wear are very very embarrassing and I think full length dressing gowns, down to the ankle, ought to be supplied.

2. Did the test I had include a test for cancer?

3. What types of cancer do they look for? Also I do not think I had a heart x-ray.

I wonder if you could answer me these questions.

Yours faithfully,

SPIKE MILLIGAN

BUPA Medical Centre

BUPA Medical Centre Limited
Webb House, 210 Pentonville Road
King's Cross, London 9TA
Telephone 01-278 4651

Director: Dr. H. B. Wright MB. FRCS

SK/VEB

6th May, 1971

Dear Mr. Milligan,

Thank you for your letter and the helpful suggestions that you have made.

We find the problem of dressing-gowns an ever recurring source of difficulty. People either complain that they are too short or too long and it seems impossible to be able to suit everybody.

As you know, there is no specific test which can exclude cancer. However, the blood tests that you have sometimes give an indication of this and yours were, of course, quite normal. The x-ray of your chest is a very good screening for cancer of the lung and sometimes the straight x-ray of the abdomen can give an indication of abnormality.

You had an x-ray of your heart and also an electrocardiograph which gives evidence of heart disease and these were both normal in your case.

I hope this satisfactorily answers your questions and once again may I thank you for having taken the trouble to write to us. It is constructive criticism such as yours which enables us to improve our service.

Yours sincerely,

Sidney Kay, M.D.,
Medical Director

S. Milligan, Esq.,

Dear Dr Kay,

Thank you for your letter of 6th May.

I think I can sort out your problem of the dressing-gowns. Why not have one long and one short dressing gown in each cubicle.

Sincerely,

SPIKE MILLIGAN

BUPA Medical Centre

BUPA Medical Centre Limited
Webb House, 210 Pentonville Road
King's Cross, London 9TA
Telephone 01-278 4651

Director: Dr. H. B. Wright MB, FRCS

SK/VEB

10th May, 1971

Dear Mr. Milligan,

Thank you very much for your excellent suggestion. It may create some difficulties with people who are what are described of as average size. However, I will certainly tell our receptionist to ask people if they would particularly like a long or a short dressing gown and try to suit them accordingly.

I made myself very ill laughing at the repeat of your programme on television the other night and am not a little disappointed that when you were here we did not diagnose that you are suffering from "earthquakes" in the very early stages of this very serious condition:

Yours sincerely,

Sidney Kay

Sidney Kay, M.D.,
Medical Director

S. Milligan, Esq.,

Dear Dr Kay,

Do you know that most average sizes of people are tall or short? I
think that the size you should have is average, tall or short,
dressing gowns which would fit everybody.

I have just been to Naples to see Vesuvius and would you believe
it the bloody fools have let it go out.

Sincerely,

SPIKE MILLIGAN

BUPA Medical Centre

BUPA Medical Centre Limited
Webb House, 210 Pentonville Road
King's Cross, London 9TA
Telephone 01-278 4651

Director: Dr. H. B. Wright MB. FRCS

SK/VEB

19th May, 1971

Dear Mr. Milligan,

Thank you once again for your helpful note.

We have given the matter further consideration and decided that probably our best course is to tackle patients' knees. It seems to us that some form of knee disguise may well prove to be a most effective answer and avoid all embarrassment. If they were not recognisable as knees then people would not really worry as to what they were seeing.

How unfortunate for you to have been to see Naples and to have found Vesuvius out!

Yours sincerely,

Sidney Kay

Sidney Kay, M.D.,
Medical Director

S. Milligan, Esq.,

Dear Dr Kay,

The Case of the Difficult Dressing Gowns

The knees' disguise is all very well but supposing somebody walks around the back, what then? Oh no, sir, if the knee is to be disguised and the back of the knee left in existence a false plastic knee will have to be fitted to the back of the leg to prevent an optical illusion when the man has his legs in the reverse position to his body. But then, the moment he kneels down for his cholesterol count the whole game is given away and the knee disguise revealed for what it is, a flagrant forgery. No, I propose that we have floor length dressing gowns and then a 2 ft dwarf will be inserted in the wearer's insteps to give the impression of mobility.

I hope this is all clear to you – I have opened a file called 'The BUPA Affair'.

Good news. As you know, they have transferred the fire from Vesuvius to Mt. Etna which is working beautifully. Book now for the third San Francisco, due any minute.

Sincerely,

SPIKE MILLIGAN

BUPA Medical Centre

BUPA Medical Centre Limited
Webb House, 210 Pentonville Road
King's Cross, London 9TA
Telephone 01-278 4051

Director: Dr. H. B. Wright MB. FRCS

SK/VEB

27th May, 1971

Dear Mr. Milligan,

Since receiving your letter of the 21st, we have been attacked by a devastating epidemic of disappearing knees. The pathetic high pitched cries of the knees as they despairingly slip out of sight is terribly heartrending. We have brought in large numbers of 9' dwarfs to try and deal with this catastrophic situation, all to no avail. We eagerly await your next helpful suggestion.....

And now for a look at the weather in the South East, over to Jack Scott in the London Weather Centre.

With kind regards,

Yours sincerely,

Sidney Kay

<u>Sidney Kay, M.D.,</u>
Medical Director

S. Milligan, Esq.,

Governors E.F. Webb MBE (Chairman) H.S. Axton FCA (Deputy Chairman) E.D. Roberts FCIS (Executive Governor) Sir Richard Powell Bt. MC O.J. Rowell J.F. Staddon FCA ATII

Spike and Peter jet-setting in San Moritz

Spike Concerned

Spike asked Roy Jenkins to help an American girl – Marylyn Zipes – who'd had a job in England and wanted to stay in spite of the fact that her visa had expired. Roy Jenkins solved the problem

14th June, 1976

Dear Mr Jenkins,

A belated thank you for helping in the case of the American girl – Marylyn Zipes. A little poem:

> It's not every day that we
> Are helped by a kindly old M.P.

Love, light and peace,

SPIKE MILLIGAN

And yet it happened again

To: The Rt Hon Roy Jenkins

1st July, 1976

My God, it's happened to me again. Another one of life's sad cases has come across my horizon.

Recently you helped me with an American girl who wanted to stay here and work, this time it's a Polish girl. For God's sake don't think these are a series of mistresses.

This young lady I found crying in a greengrocery store, and being a compassionate person I asked what the trouble was. She's Polish, was studying over here, then found the financial going was hard, stopped being a student and illegally went to work in the greengrocers in Moscow Road.

The shop changed hands and the elderly lady who runs the shop reported her to the Police for working without a permit. All in all as a result of this her case comes up in August, as to whether she stays in the country or leaves. But, the girl is heartbroken as she is in love (and in this weather who can blame her), and it's on the strength of her romantic attachment that I am writing to ask you to consider her staying here.

She told me she likes living here and is not happy with the political climate in her own country, so dear Roy Jenkins, over to you.

Her name is Marika Kuna, she currently lives at Craven Hill Gardens, London W2. but she is moving to Aylestone Avenue, London NW6.

I must say here and now that my career as an Assistant Home Secretary will terminate after this particular case, I don't intend to do this sort of thing anymore.

Something on a happier note, I got a handful of bird seed and put it in a flower pot, and good God, I now have sunflowers, isn't that lovely?

Love, light and peace,

SPIKE MILLIGAN

To : His Holiness The Pope,
The Vatican

21st October, 1976

Your Holiness,

A couple of years ago I wrote to you regarding a Professor White in America who carries out awful experiments on animals, and I said unless the Church could make a definite decision about excommunication or not, that I myself could not go on being a Catholic whilst such a crime was being committed.

My letter was eventually passed to Cardinal Heenan who wrote to me, alas with no positive decision about what the Church should do. In the face of this, I have decided I cannot be a Catholic any longer.

I wish to take up the Buddhist Faith.

I have the Honour to remain,
your Holiness's most devoted and
obedient servant.

SPIKE MILLIGAN

In reply, Spike had a noncommittal answer from John Crowley at Archbishop's House, London

Dear Mr Crowley,

Thank you for your letter, but it doesn't do anything positive.
Years ago I reported the horrendous experiments of Professor
White, and I feel helpless in the face of these so called 'scientific
experiments', and when I discovered the man was a Catholic, I
was horrified some approach had not been made to him by a
Catholic in an authoritarian position. He should be ex-
communicated, alas he hasn't been and my efforts to bring
pressure on him, via the Church, have failed and, therefore, it's
no good staying with a very large Regiment, holding rifles, when
none of them, in fact, have any ammunition.

Therefore, I intend to withdraw from the Roman Catholic faith;
it's a very sad decision to make, but as Hamlet once said 'a good
idea must give way to a better one' and my better one will be
Buddhism.

Thanks for writing.

Sincerely,

SPIKE MILLIGAN

Dear Harold Wilson,

I was glad to know that the proposed debate on John Stonehouse has been cancelled.

We all realise the extent of the social and political implications of his actions in the past year, but I fear that all this is the result of a slowly degenerating mental condition, and I speak as one who has been wrestling with this problem most of my life.

What has happened is Stonehouse had tried to enter into a financial empire, by various negotiations, but failed, as many people do, but was of such mental condition that he was unable to face the consequences, and quite obviously the attempt to make out he was dead and start life under a different name, is not the work of a criminal, but the work of a man who just mentally does not have the wherewithal to face up to it, and this is not a criminal personality, but that of somebody who was mentally never suited to the stresses and strains of high international finance. Of course, the quality of this psychic personality only became manifest when faced with this sudden Sword of Damocles which he had not bargained for.

One only has to see television films of him, and to hear his statements to realise that he is in absolutely no fit state to face up to a political enquiry, and to be followed by court cases involving finance, it would be best to show the quality of humanity in our politics to re-consider what lines to take in relationship to how very ill he is, and I fear, who might eventually end up in a mental home.

No need to answer this letter as I know how busy you are, but I assure you I speak to you after great consideration and experiences in mental problems.

Love, light and peace,

SPIKE MILLIGAN

P.S. I see you sent Tony Benn sideways.

Dear Laurence,

This is to let you know that I morally support the miners in their fight for higher wages. During the war there were several Geordie miners in my regiment and I grew to like and eventually love them for their tremendous courage, sense of humour and unfailing loyalty.

When I read that a bank made £170M profit last year and that an oil company made £241M tax-free profit the year before, I cannot see how any government except for an immoral one would refuse the men a rise.

Good luck with your fight. If there is anything I can do please let me know.

Sincerely,

SPIKE MILLIGAN

P.S. One time member of the Transport and General Workers Union.

Dear Lads,

This is to let you know that you have my full support in asking for better conditions and wages from your bosses. For too long, stable lads have been used almost in the same context as Victorian workers were, and you can see what a lot of bastards the public are when they try to do you up at the races. I wonder, if they are so patriotic on keeping wages down, why they were not all at work that day, themselves.

Anyway, good luck to you all.

Regards,

SPIKE MILLIGAN

TRANSPORT & GENERAL WORKERS' UNION

Registered Office:
TRANSPORT HOUSE,
SMITH SQUARE, LONDON, S.W.1.
Gen. Sec.: J. L. JONES, M.B.E.
Asst. Gen. Sec.: C. H. URWIN

"WOODBERRY",
213 GREEN LANES,
FINSBURY PARK,
LONDON, N.4 2 HB.

Please reply to:
BEVAN HOUSE,
CAMPS ROAD, HAVERHILL,
SUFFOLK, CB9 8HF.
TELEPHONE: HAVERHILL 5773

REGION No. 1
(London and Home Counties)

Regional Secretary: B. FRY
Telephone: 01-800 4261/7

Your Ref.:

Please quote Ref. No

Our Ref.: SH/JAC/650

11th July, 1975.

DISTRICT OFFICE
COMMUNICATION

Mr. Spike Milligan,

Dear Mr. Milligan,

It was indeed a pleasure to receive your letter of support for the action being taken by the Newmarket Stablelads to secure better wages and conditions in an Industry that is still being run on a Dickensian basis.

Having read your letter to the Lads at a meeting held in Newmarket last evening, it was encouraging to see how your letter of support boosted their moral especially having learned that most of the lads on official strike had received their cards through the post that very morning, and others had been given notice of eviction from their hostels and tied accomodation by the Newmarket Trainers who are adamant to maintain their feudal approach in dealing with staff.

The Lads have asked me to convey their appreciation for your letter of support.

Yours sincerely,

S, Horncastle,
DISTRICT OFFICIAL

This is an example of the kind of letter he writes in an effort to help the mentally depressed

7th November 1973

Dear Mark,

I have just received your letter as I have been away and it was waiting for me on my desk when I returned. You seem to be in a state and first things first. You say you need money badly, O.K. I am enclosing herewith £10 to try and help. Of course money is not going to cure your illness and giving you money is not going to get you a job.

You must try and accept the fact that you are a sick person and that you have a condition and whereas it will become very oppressive at times and cause you great mental anguish and difficulty especially in your home life, you have to accept the fact that you must do something about it.

  1) I suggest you accept the fact that you are ill and you might have to live with it, and

  2) You will go up and down emotionally but it will not kill you.

This means you need a job which does not demand too much mental stress. Working on a farm can have its compensations especially working with animals who are depending on you rather than you depending on them. Working with lots of people will obviously be difficult for you.

I am certain that nobody is going to turn you away from doing some farm work if you explain the position to the farmer in question. I am certain there is such a shortage of labour on the land that you should get some sort of a job on a farm and it need only be for a short period.

  a) To stabilize yourself.

  b) Get a few pounds in to pay the rent.

I am sorry I cannot do more than this. I am only human and get a lot of stress myself and have to keep getting off the floor and I try and keep going and many is the time that I just have to back away.

Let me know how you are by the time you get this letter. Of course you know you are allowed to get Social Security so you and your family should not starve even though it can be very tight. Try and seek a little comfort and think of the 150,000 who have just died of starvation in Ethiopia.

Anyhow let me know how you get on.

Love, Light and Peace,

SPIKE

P.S. Driving fast at walls is very bad for you.

These sort of things only happen to Spike – he was working at London Weekend Television and an outside line had been left in his dressing room. A girl was ringing a TV station to see if anyone could help her – and he was immediately involved

To: G. Angel, Esq,
Private Office of The Home Office   *8th September 1971*

Dear Mr Angel,

I am committing the facts of the telephone call I received to paper. Briefly it's this.

The girl's name is Sheila Kuar. She is living at Derby Road, Nottingham. She told me she had been born in Grimsby and was now seventeen years of age and of the Sikh religion. She left school nine months ago and since then has not been allowed to leave the house. Yesterday she was engaged to a man she has not yet seen and is to marry in six months' time. The girl told me this in a very emotional state, occasionally breaking down and crying. She told me she did not wish to marry this man and would rather live a life of her own, but at the same time she was very frightened of imparting this knowledge to anybody, which might result in her father or mother finding out she had made this telephone call asking for help.

I questioned her again and again and it would seem to me that this was a bona fide case of a subservient daughter who has seen English life and wants to live one like other English girls. But now, being tied to her parents' religion and being forced to stay indoors and likewise marry a man she does not wish to, I promised her that I would not do anything without asking her permission.

There is the case as it stands.

I think, as you suggested on the telephone, it would be best if the police authority in Nottingham were informed by you of the situation and takes a course of action to allow the girl freedom without incurring the wrath of her parents, for having imparted this information to the authorities so it will be a case for the police to use great tact and care so as not to cause suspicion on the girl.

She further added that there were quite a number of other Pakistani and Sikh girls in the same area, all of whom were being forced to undergo the ritual I have already mentioned.

If there is any way I can help I myself will do so.

Love, light and peace,

SPIKE

I know the Home Office took up the case but I do not know the outcome

1

Pauline Jones was sent to prison for abducting a baby out of love – not for money

25th January, 1972

Dear Pauline Jones,

I am just writing to tell you that I don't think that you should be put in any kind of prison, I think it very cruel that they should do this to you, and many thousands of people think the same. I admit you must have given great mental anguish to the parents but you were so desperate to love something that you did not think of that.

If there is anything I can get you while you are in prison like books or magazines, do let me know.

Love, Light and Peace,

SPIKE MILLIGAN

2

He could not find out if she received his letters or not. He wrote to several people including Miss Morgan – the Governor of the prison

22nd March, 1972

Dear Miss Morgan,

Thank you for your letter of the 17th March.

I cannot help thinking this is ambiguous in that, and I quote, 'Pauline Jones received all the correspondence she was entitled to'. Therefore, was my correspondence among that which she was entitled to? If not, what happens to a letter written to a prisoner, to which she is not entitled – is the letter destroyed or is it returned to the sender?

All I am trying to do is to make contact with this girl to try and help her, and I am sure you will agree that this is a good thing. So in trying to help her I am seeking your help to inform me as to whether she received my letter, and has she read it.

You do appreciate my approach is a humanitarian one and your reply did not answer my question in my first letter. So I wonder if you could be more specific. It is very simple to say yes or no, because if she has not received my letter quite obviously I must write to her again.

Once again, this can only be done when I have received sufficient information from you.

Sincerely,

SPIKE MILLIGAN

3

He persisted

23rd March, 1972

Dear Pauline,

I have already written one letter to you but you may not have got it because, as you mentioned in the press, you were not getting all the mail you should.

I wrote to the Governor of Askham Grange who answered me in ambiguous terms saying you had got all the mail you were entitled to. So I am writing again in the hopes that you get this letter.

I wrote saying that I disagreed entirely with having you put away in any kind of Institution, and I believe you should have a home atmosphere with lots of love and understanding and tolerance. I still believe this to be the case and I said so specifically on 'Speak Easy' last Sunday and everybody in the audience agreed with me. If you do get this letter I beg of you to answer it just so I know that you have got it. I will keep writing to you until I get an answer.

If you cannot write to me, can you ask one of your prison visitors to telephone me at London and tell me whether you are getting any mail from me?

If there is anything I can do to help you in any way please let me know and I will do my best.

Love, Light, and Peace,

SPIKE MILLIGAN

To: *The Governor,*
H.M. Prison,
Styal   *29th September, 1972*

Dear Sir,

Here is a book of poems that I would like to give to Pauline Jones. However, I believe there are prison rules which sometimes restrict the handing on of books or presents to persons. If this should be the case, I should like the book to be returned to me in the attached envelope. Though for the love of me I cannot imagine what possible harm the book can do to the prison system, other than make it more human.

Respectfully,

SPIKE MILLIGAN

Finally he managed to make contact with her, and received several letters from her. Here are two of the letters he wrote to her

5th July 1972

My dear Pauline,

Owing to pressure of work I am dictating this letter to you, whereas I would prefer to write it by hand. We are living in a mad world.

I was delighted to see that, rather than sitting around feeling sorry for yourself, you have got stuck into something called by that good old name 'work'. Believe me, Pauline, people are not very fond of work these days, but usually those people are miserable and dissatisfied because of that very reason.

My Mother is 78 now, she gets up at 6.30 in the morning and three days a week she goes to Mass, she cleans the house herself, washes all the sheets by hand, looks after the garden and makes jam preserves, and I really don't know of a happier woman.

I myself when I am very depressed work as hard as I can and as well as I can, and but for that I think I would go mad. So remember this as a fellow neurotic work is almost Godlike.

The fact you have learned to crochet and upholster means that if you cared to you could set yourself up in one room and sell it to the numerous boutiques that are springing up in London that are looking for quality work and unusual items.

Five months and nine days, of course, seems a long time to somebody in prison, and to somebody outside not long at all, this quite obviously is a frame of mind under certain circumstances. Actually it is the same time both inside and outside prison, so you have to gear your mind to working hard and looking forward to starting work the next morning, and perhaps keeping a small diary at night of life in prison with a view to possibly selling it to a newspaper or magazine when you get out, it will all help time to pass quickly.

I realise, as you say, that the conversation might be at a very low ebb, but that in itself is worth observing and recording as a life experience which going to a school would not teach you.

I hope your Father is in touch with you regularly.

You have never told me what your feelings were about taking the baby, I would love to talk to you about it sometime. As a person who is interested in lame dogs (being one myself), if you find out what the problem is you can often find a cure, or at least a crutch to help the person along.

Let me tell you that the weather on the outside of prison is just as bloody awful as it is on the inside at the moment.

I am at present trying to write a Fairy Story for children in longhand and finding it very difficult not to make mistakes, but I like a challenge.

I have not any more news to convey to you, so keep your chin up girl, the world is a bloody awful place – it always will be, and as long as you approach it with that in mind, you don't get so many disappointments.

Love, Light and Peace,

SPIKE MILLIGAN

P.S. If there is anything I can send you please let me know, like books, newspapers, or a man.

My dear Pauline,

Thank you for your letter. I really don't understand this stupid idea of not letting you see all your mail properly. I cannot see what possible harm can be done by a person receiving a letter. I used to think Her Majesty's mail was inviolate. What it means is that it is a breach of privilege and privacy to which I would never subscribe even if I belonged to the police. I hope that this letter is being read by you and not by a policeman.

I don't suppose that at this stage the campaign to try and get you out before time will bear fruit, primarily because the creature called homo sapiens, of which the Home Secretary is one, is completely immovable when it comes to considering human patterns on a psychiatric level. What I mean is if the Home Secretary has never suffered mental stress which has caused mental breakdown, he just does not understand the language or the problem of the person, who is, in this case, you. I have just managed to get a girl away from two monstrous psychiatrists at Guys Hospital, who had driven her to the stage where she was going to commit suicide. Fortunately I got her out and passed her into the hands of a human being and now she is safe. So don't expect the world to be a better or a worse place when you come out. Nothing has changed – nothing will ever change because man is unchangeable.

No matter what laws are passed there are always the people who will act upon them, witness the ordinary German soldier who was told to shoot Jews, women and children as well, and did it because that was the law.

Where are you going when you come out of prison? Are you going to stay with your father? Don't forget I would like to see you once or twice when you come out. Please remember no matter what the conditions are in prison or what they make you do, it is not a permanency, it is going to end shortly, and with that in mind try and take whatever they give you with a degree of rationality, after all, you are an intelligent girl and I think it is within your means to do it. I agree, passing in a pyjama factory must be soul destroying, but as I say, remember it is coming to an end.

116

I am sending you a copy of my book of poems called Small
Dreams of a Scorpion. I am enclosing an envelope for its return,
that is if the prison authorities won't let you have it. I am asking
them to return it to me at once and I will keep it for you until you
come out. I am sending the book care of the prison Governor as I
don't want it to get lost. I am asking him to either give it to you
or send it to me back, nothing in between will do.

I am flying to Australia to see my mother and brother in a few
days' time. I will be away for a month. If you write to me care of
my office they will forward any letters on to me.

Love, light and peace,

SPIKE MILLIGAN

Where the hell did he park his car?

The Dog Shit Affair

To : The Superintendent,
Police Station,
Harrow Road,
London W2   19th April, 1972

Dear Sir,

I want to report an incident.

On Sunday 2nd April, 1972, at approximately 4.30 pm. I
witnessed two women and a man with a Great Dane dog – the
dog defecated on the pavement.

I followed the people who went to Queens Mews.

I wrote to the Westminster City Council and they told me I
should report the incident to the Police.

As the streets of Bayswater are polluted excessively by this
disgusting habit I do hope we can prosecute.

                                        Respectfully,

                                SPIKE MILLIGAN

To: Inspector Haines,
Harrow Road Police Station,
London W2   *16th May, 1972*

Dear Sir,

> *Milligan versus Dog Shit*
> *Case Number 2.*

On Sunday the 7th May at about 11.30 am. a large black dog
defecated on the pavement, I called the creature and said 'Come
here Darling', and saw that its label bore the address – Burnham
Court, Moscow Road, and the dog's name was Liz. A fitting
Royal name for a debasement of the Royal city.

Would you please prosecute?

Sincerely,

SPIKE MILLIGAN

	To:	SPIKE MILLIGAN.
	Copy to:	
From NORMA FARNES		
	Date:	31/5/72

Ref.:

Subject:

INSPECTOR HAINES FROM HARROW ROAD POLICE STATION CALLED IN TO
SEE YOU TODAY REGARDING THE LETTER YOU SENT HIM 'MILLIGAN VERSUS
DOG SHIT CASE NO. 2.'.

HE PERSONALLY IS GOING ALONG TO BURNHAM COURT TO SEE THE OWNERS OF
THE DOG LIZ. AND GIVE THEM A WARNING. HE SAID HE THOUGHT IT BEST
TO GO AND GIVE THEM A WARNING WITHOUT PROSECUTING FIRST. BECAUSE
YOU WOULD HAVE TO GO TO COURT AND GIVE EVIDENCE, AND HE THOUGHT IT
BEST TO GIVE THEM A WARNING. HOWEVER, IF YOU WANT TO PROSECUTE
WILL YOU CONTACT HIM.

No don't prosecute – but do warn.
What about Dog Shit No 1?

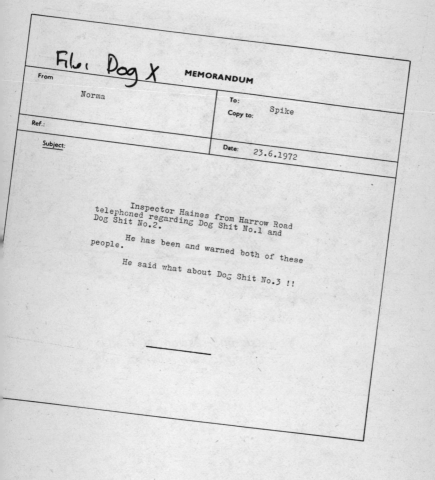

File, Dog X

MEMORANDUM

From

Norma

To:

Copy to: Spike

Ref.:

Subject:

Date: 23.6.1972

      Inspector Haines from Harrow Road telephoned regarding Dog Shit No.1 and Dog Shit No.2.

      He has been and warned both of these people.

      He said what about Dog Shit No.3 !!

123

Spike signing session – Canada
Trying to earn a living

Spike and
the Lamp Posts

12th February, 1968

Dear Lord Kennet,

As you know, the latest bureaucratic vandals have been let loose on Constitution Hill, and needlessly so.

One look at the modified lamp standards in Regents Park shows that there was no need to put up those great bent iron fingers which are out of proportion, even with the trees.

Would you like to tell me why it was not possible to carry out modifications to gas lamps on Constitution Hill, as per Regents Park?

I presume that this is a matter of regions, and the cretins who put up lights in Constitution Hill just don't know the existence of the gas lamps in Regents Park, being so splendidly adapted to modern circumstances.

I can't wait to see the plastic crocuses.

Dejectedly,

SPIKE MILLIGAN

12th February, 1968

Dear Anthony Greenwood,

I don't know how it has come about but scenic mayhem has been committed on Constitution Hill, and you know what I mean.

If you were to walk in Regents Park after dark, you will notice that the gas lamps there have been beautifully modified to take, what in essence, looks like gas lights, but is, in fact, very clever electricity adaptation.

Why can this be carried out in Regents Park, and Constitution Hill has to have those iron gallows?

I really am utterly horrified; I have driven up and down Constitution Hill by gas light for five years, and never seen an accident.

Cannot you have second thoughts about this?

Respectfully,

SPIKE MILLIGAN

To: The Rt Hon Anthony Greenwood, MP

4th March, 1968

Dear Tony,

If the rumours I hear are true, then it's great news about the lamps.

Believe me, it will pay off in the end, because one day it will be the only gas lit street in Europe, and tourists *pay* money to see things like this.

Now then, I am going to help Britain; if you supply me with black gunmetal paint, and outdoor gold leaf paint, I will gather together volunteers who will make these lamp posts beautiful, and as delightful as they were when originally painted.

I would pay for the paint myself, but having spent £350 on restoring the Elfin Oak Tree, I asked for tax relief from the Min. of Mon. (Ministry of Money), and they said 'No'.

Anyhow, give me the go ahead, and I will spend the summer making these lamp posts one of the delights of London.

Sincerely,

SPIKE MILLIGAN

LAMBETH BRIDGE HOUSE
LONDON. S.E.1

12th March, 1968.

M.O. 2183/3

P. Preservation dd Buildings file

S

Dear Spike

Anthony Greenwood has sent me your letter of 4th March about the lamp standards on Constitution Hill as I am responsible for the management of the Royal Parks.

As I announced in the House of Commons on 26th February, I have decided to remove the new electric standards, retain the old standards, and carry out experiments to see how the best standard of lighting can be achieved in Constitution Hill.

It is very good of you to offer to find volunteers to join you in painting the old standards. Now, however, that these standards are to remain, we shall ourselves be setting about restoring them to a presentable condition in the near future.

I hope that you will not think I am being ungracious if I do not accept your generous offer. It is probable that a certain amount of metal repair work will need to be done, and I think it would be preferable if this and the painting of the standards were done in the normal way under Ministry arrangements.

Sincerely

Bob Mellish

R. J. MELLISH

Don't get mad + keep away from T.V. !!

Spike Milligan, Esq.

Come + have + chat + a drink Bob.

129

Dear Lads,

Regarding the now historic lamp posts in Constitution Hill.

All right then, go ahead and get them painted, but I beg you to take note of the method in which the ironwork round Buckingham Palace has been painted. Whosoever did it, knew exactly the correct way to paint regal ironwork.

If left to a man with a paint-pot and a brush then I fear the lamp posts could be painted an agonised green, brown or in some cases, believe it or not, blue.

Can I assure you that they must be gunmetal black and gilding all embossments.

I am trying to do my duty as a citizen, in pointing these things out because as you may, or may not, know, this country is not noted for respecting its minor works of art, although we spend millions restoring Windsor Castle, using Fine Arts Commission; but early Regency lamp posts, which are every bit as beautiful and delicate and gracefully designed, are by-passed.

So please assure me what method and who is going to paint them.

I demand my rights as a citizen.

                                        Semi loyal subject,

                                        SPIKE MILLIGAN

The iron fingers were taken down and the Victorian lamps remained
I telephoned Mr Robert Mellish to ask him permission to reproduce his letter in this book.
He was one of the most charming and helpful people I had contacted and he did ask me especially to say:
'Had it not been for Spike Milligan, these lamp posts would not be here today.'

Spike Mischievous

Will be present at the Reception
for Dr. Billy Graham at the Kensington
Palace Hotel on Saturday, 25th
August 1973 at 11.00 p.m.

I dont think this man is holy —
he has religious Paranoia — and
thats a different thing.

Keith Michel telephoned and asked Spike to contribute to the show 'In Order of Appearance' at Chichester Festival Theatre. He was asked to contribute a sonnet or anything on his favourite King or Queen of England.

Spike sent a song about Henry VIII and his wives. The manuscript came back with the comment that Catherine Parr was not included. I sent the compliment slip to Spike and wrote the comment 'Catherine Parr is missing.' Below is the result

TYPE
(S) (1 copy
me)
Chichester
Festival Theatre
CATHERINE PARR IS
MISSING. TALK TO
ME. No. Call the
Police.
With compliments

TEL. 01-499-9000   AMERICAN EMBASSY, LONDON

FOR PUBLICATION - WITH OR WITHOUT ATTRIBUTION

INFO

Wednesday,
June 21st, 1972

CORRECTION KISSINGER Q & A TEXT

In the 5th paragraph on page 1 of a Dr. Henry Kissinger
briefing text sent to you on Monday, June 19th, the
figure of 1,168 is mentioned in regard to an estimate
of Soviet missiles currently deployed.

This figure should be: 1,618

- - - - - -

. Oh what a relief!

To : Dr Philip H. Moore   *27th March, 1972*

Dear Dr Moore,

How dare you send me a bill. I was conscious throughout the
operation and my screams were recorded as far away as
Houndsditch.

Signed : Bottomless Milligan

P.S. Charge me all that money, you must think my purse is
bottomless, well it's not anymore.

To : The Editor,
Rand Daily Mail,
Johannesburg   *20th August, 1976*

Sir,

I have just received an incredible cutting from your newspaper,
showing two porcupines, one called Spike and one called
Milligan.

You realise that this has turned me into a bisexual schizophrenic.

You will be hearing from my solicitor in the morning.

                                        Sincerely,

                                SPIKE MILLIGAN

P.S. My solicitor is called Harry Secombe, and he is two
Aardvark.

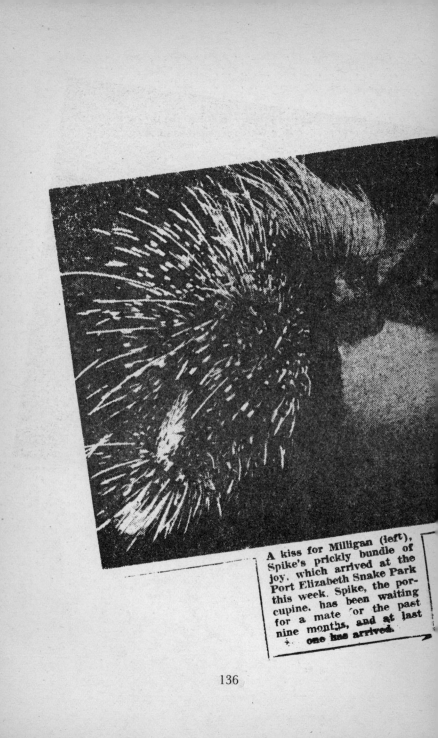

A kiss for Milligan (left), Spike's prickly bundle of joy, which arrived at the Port Elizabeth Snake Park this week. Spike, the porcupine, has been waiting for a mate 'or the past nine months, and at last one has arrived.

Club Oenologique Wine & Spirit Judge

1972

This Diploma affirms that

Spike Milligan Esq.

has passed the Club Oenologique examination

and is hereby awarded the Gold *insignia*
This means I've got pissed more times than
the Chairman.

Director
Club Oenologique

Chairman
Club Oenologique

Spike and the
Rest of the World

To: *Leslie Frewin, Esq.*
Leslie Frewin Publishers Ltd.   *19th June, 1972*

Dear Leslie,

I was refused a publicity copy of 'VALENTINO', and I
wanted it with a view to making a film. They said on strict orders
you did not give away free 'VALENTINOs'.

Now then, Sonny Jim, if you give me a free copy of the book you
might make a lot of money out of the film.

Come on now, stop hiding in the flat counting your money, send
me a free copy and – Voila.

                                        Sincerely,

                                        SPIKE

A Mr Stephen Gard wrote complaining about Spike's book
'Monty'. He said that he had come to the conclusion that
Spike detested the army. This is Spike's reply

                                        28th February, 1977

Dear Stephen,

Questions, questions, questions – if you are disappointed in my
book 'MONTY', so am I. I must be more disappointed than
you because I spent a year collecting material for it, and it was a
choice of having it made into a suit or a book.

There are lots of one liners in the book, but then when the
German Army are throwing bloody great lumps of hot iron at
you, one only has time for one liners, in fact, the book should
really consist of the following:

140

'Oh fuck'

'Look out'

'Christ here's another'

'Where did that fall'?

'My lorry's on fire'

'Oh Christ, the cook is dead'.

You realise a book just consisting of those would just be the end, so my one liners are extensions of these brevities.

Then you are worried because as yet I have not mentioned my meeting with Secombe and later Sellers, well by the end of the Monty book I had as yet not met either Secombe or Sellers. I met Secombe in Italy, which will be in vol 4, and I am arranging to meet Peter Sellers on page 78 in vol 5 in London. I'm sorry I can't put back the clock to meet Secombe in 1941, to alleviate your disappointment – hope springs anew with the information I have given you.

Another thing that bothers you is 'cowardice in the face of the enemy'. Well, the point is I suffer from cowardice in the face of the enemy throughout the war – in the face of the enemy, also in the legs, the elbows, and the wrists, in fact, after two years in the front line a mortar bomb exploded by my head (or was it my head exploded by a mortar bomb), and it so frightened me, I put on a tremendous act of stammering, stuttering, and shivering. This mixed with cries of 'mother' and a free flow of dysentery enabled me to be taken out of the line and down-graded to B2. But for that brilliant performance, this letter would be coming to you from a grave in Italy.

Any more questions from you and our friendship is at an end.

Sincerely,

SPIKE MILLIGAN

141

Dear Sir,

re – *The Origin of the Black Stump*

The following is the true origin of the name in question.

Among Captain Cook's crew who landed in Australia, was a Dr Thompson who had a wooden leg. The first night ashore, a large bonfire was built, around which slept Cook and the members of his crew. Alas, Dr Thompson slept with his wooden leg too near the fire and it ignited; by dawn the wooden leg was charred and burnt, hence the name 'The Black Stump'.

I Spike Milligan being of sound mind do hereby swear this story to be true as I was present at it on that fateful morning.

Signed   *SPIKE MILLIGAN*

P.S. To-morrow is my 219th Birthday and the Commonwealth Savings Bank of Australia are giving me a handsome clock which only has the figure 10 on it and on the stroke of 10 a Bank Manager pops out of the front and says 'The time is 10 o'clock and the Commonwealth Savings Bank is open for business'.

To: *Miss Cleo Laine*   *20th June, 1972*

Dear Cleo,

You were fantastic last night, I was going to send you Champagne but after the way you sparkled it was pointless.

Love, Light, and Peace,

SPIKE

P.S. It was also expensive.
P.P.S. My regards to that man who conducts the band for you.

To: *Sir Hugh Fraser,*
Harrods Ltd.   *1st March, 1965*

Sir,

A year ago I bought a safety ladder from your firm. It was jolly good and it remained very safe as long as I kept tightening up the nuts and screws on it and using another ladder.

I have recently explained in detail to one of your safety ladder men that the amount that you would have to pay me if I broke my neck would go into thousands. Now I don't want to see you but could you try and arrange for the ladder to be taken away, inspect it and the two offending bolts which keep falling off replaced so they don't unscrew? I am not going to charge you anything for the time I spend writing these letters and the time I spend telephoning up your departments but you are lucky I don't.

Yours faithfully,

SPIKE MILLIGAN

To : Bill Lyddon Esq.,
BMC   *21st September, 1967*

Dear Mr Lyddon,

This is a matter of honour. I recently took charge of a Mini Cooper
S which immediately overheated on the M 1. Consequently I had to
have it towed to Northampton, and paid for the hire of a private car
to Birmingham. There was no guarantee when the car would be
ready so my secretary had to bring her car for me to use whilst I was
there. Expenses were incurred for her return to London.

My secretary collected the car and then drove it to Newcastle where
we changed cars. All in all about £20 was incurred in expenses.

It didn't stop there; I had trouble in Scotland, and also in Coventry
where I had to hire a car. I then wrote a furious letter to the
Chairman, Sir George Harriman, and as a result I managed to get
a loan of a car whilst my car was being repaired. All in all it was a bit
of a sickener.

Now I don't want any of this money returned, but I had a thought.
I am flying out to Australia this Monday and I thought perhaps
your Company would feel better if you could arrange to loan me a
car, a Mini Minor for the three weeks I am in Sydney. If your
Agents out there would like to contact me I shall be at Woy Woy,
NSW, Australia.

Yours faithfully,

SPIKE MILLIGAN

BMC wrote and said they would try to see what they could arrange – they managed to arrange nothing, so:

31st January, 1968

Dear Mr Lyddon,

When in Australia I waited for BMC to, at least, get in touch with me, and say 'yes' or 'no'.

True to England, I heard nothing. Fortunately the Australians are much quicker on the ball and they loaned me a Holden. The publicity for both of us was very nice.

Thank you, for what I don't know.

Sincerely,

SPIKE MILLIGAN

BMC apologised and this was Spike's comment at the end of their letter

Im backing Britain –
over a cliff.

there should be a file for useless
letters - as

Worldwide Service for
Austin, Austin Commercial, Austin-Healey, MG, Morris, Morris-Commercial, Riley, Vanden Plas, Wolseley, Nuffield Tractor

ARCHAEOLOGICAL INSTITUTE OF AMERICA

260 West Broadway
New York, New York 10013

Date _January 10_

Dear _Mr. Milligan_

Thank you for your recent order/renewal for:

___X___ a subscription to ARCHAEOLOGY

_____ a subscription to THE AMERICAN JOURNAL OF ARCHAEOLOGY

_____ membership in the Institute (Type of membership: _____)

_____

As you can see from the information we are enclosing, the cost of the above
was increased as of January 1, 1970.

Instead of holding your check and awaiting additional payment, which may
cause unnecessary delay and possible confusion, we are returning it to you.
Would you be kind enough to send us a new check in the correct amount.
Upon receipt we will immediately process your order.

Please direct your reply to my attention. Thank you.

Sincerely,

Lisa Vives
Subscription & Membership
Secretary

P.S. I think you're terrific.

146

To: *Miss Lisa Vives,*
The Archaeological Institute of America   *12th January, 1972*

Dear Lisa,

Your P.S. made my grey morning and gave it shafts of golden
and silver that might have sprung from the face of a young
pharaoh as the dawn sun has its sarcophagus in the Valley of
Kings.

Now when you say 'P.S. I think you are terrific' are you thinking
of me in the Archaeological light, or do you believe what I do,
that I am still alive?

Love, Light, and Peace,

SPIKE MILLIGAN

St Thomas's Hospital told Spike that his son was being
supplied with gammaglobulin regularly. This was his reply:

28th November, 1973

Dear J. K. H. Rees, MB, MRCP,

Your letter of 12th Oct. 1973 with its formidable demands
(anything up to six hours a day for three months to comply), is not
on and I tell you for why chum. My wife and I have not got a son
called Desmond. However, my mother has a son called Desmond
who is my brother and he is in distant Australia chum, that is
where the gammaglobulin is going, that is why there is this great
shortage in England, I am walking around with not enough
gammaglobulin to get me to my car, in fact I am writing this
from my car as I have not enough to get back.

Respectfully,   *SPIKE MILLIGAN*

P.S. My blood pressure is very, very, low, please send blood.

Dear Mr Wilson,

I wonder if you can help? I only come to you after all for help. I have been to the solicitor, and have tried the Citizens' Advice, Consumer Advice, but no result.

Recently, I bought a Biro pen which burst in the pocket of my shirt, and ruined it. I wrote to the company, and asked will they reimburse me for the loss of the shirt, explaining that I wasn't given to trying to get free shirts in this manner. They replied and said 'There wasn't enough reason for them to reimburse me'.

As a public-minded citizen, I thought there must be some standard in this country, whereby a man who sells you a faulty pen is not allowed to get away with it scot free. There must be surely some yard stick whereby the public are protected against big time businesses, who in this case have proved to have no moral conscience at all.

Is there any way in the political scene of our country whereby a citizen can get a square deal? I am determined to see this through to my own satisfaction even if it means chucking bricks through the windows of the Biro manufacturers. This will be only a last resort.

Please help.

Sincerely,

SPIKE MILLIGAN

With receiving hundreds of letters a week, nobody can remember what happened to the shirt

A student wrote to Spike asking him to settle a discussion about the true composer of the Ying Tong Song

To: Jan Stead   *6th November, 1973*

Dear Jan,

This is to prove that beyond all question of doubt that I wrote the Ying Tong Song and that Stravinsky did not. Mind you, he does not know he did not write the Ying Tong song but I do which makes me much more enlightened than Stravinsky especially as he snuffed it a couple of years ago.

Love, Light and Peace,

SPIKE

Half wit on location –
dig the shorts –
still trying to earn a living

Ernest Todd was the New Zealand Touring Manager to
Britain during 1971/2. Spike wrote to him about
the team's visit

21st February, 1973

Dear Mr Todd,

I thought perhaps after the outrageously unfair press you got out
here, you would like to have a letter from somebody who has
played and loved Rugby all his life. I did have the pleasure of
speaking with you at the Shelbourne Hotel for a brief moment
but being Irish and having held you to a draw, I had been
celebrating. Now I am sober and would like to say that since you
have all left, the days are very dull out here and we have nothing
to talk about.

I am sure you must know in your heart that all rugby fans across
Great Britain really enjoyed your trip and all in all you gave us some
lively conversation and some great playing to talk about. Of course
there are always 'incidents' in rugby on both sides, this is because
the men that are playing it are human beings and I myself, while
only weighing 10 stone 8 lbs, as a winger, hit a 16 stone lock
forward. Now don't tell me if I had been in my right mind I would
have done that, but in the heat of the game I could not help it and
once again he made no attempt at retaliation at me which is
another part of the game which is great. So, what can I say, other
than thanks for bringing your marvellous men over and we await
your return – welcome, a thousand welcomes.

Tell Grant Batty he is a little darling. I know how he felt in the
game against the Barbarians because he really was on his way
to scoring a try when he was tackled without the ball and had he
scored that try, Joe Caram could have converted and my God
that would have set the game alight.

I for one thought the crowd were boorish to have booed him but I
don't think it was very deep rooted.

Once again, thanks for a great time.

Yours sincerely,

SPIKE MILLIGAN

And just for a change here are two letters and a telegram from guess who?

HOTEL LEOFRIC
Coventry
CV1 1LZ
Telephone Coventry 21371/5

Dear Spike

Let me place on record once again that I think that the book is wonderful. It contains all the substance of life in those days and all the compassion and comradeship of Army existence.

In other words it's Heading great!!

Very sincerely

Ned of the Valleys

Proprietor—Ind Coope Limited

Sis ist der Englische yoke ja?

3016428 Gunner Milligan T.
First Floor <u>Latrines</u>,
London, <u>W.C.1</u>.   Somvere in Berlin

Meine liebe Milligan,

    Ze Führer vos most interested to learn ov your new
volume ov var memoirs und has asked me to zank you vor your
kind invitation to attend ze booze-down (as ze Englische zo
quaintly call it).

    Unfortunately, as you vill know, Ze Führer has not been
at all vell since ze nasty incident in ze bünker und most of
ze time just lies around looking ashen. In fact we are really
quite vorried about him.

    Although he cannot be vis you on ze 7th Oktober, he has
instructed me to vish you vell und hopes zat ze book vill sell
many copies.

    In ze meantime, ze Führer understands zat he is quoted
much in ze book und vunders vot ze situation ist about ze
royalties.

    An announcement in Ze Times personal columns vill reach
him.

        Viz all gut wishes

        D! Zwartzenkopfen
        Oberleutmantgruppenführer
        Last Battalion, S.S.

152

Her dare ~~yer post~~ a ~~ise~~ her birthday
with out ~~mailing for our~~ birthday card.

TELEGRAM

Prefix   Time handed in.   Office of origin and Service Instructions.   Words.

No.

OFFICE STAMP

167

PADDINGTON
S.O.
10 SEP 74
SPRING ST W.2

At _____ m
To
By _____

RECEIVED

From _____

By _____

T/4 1430 ST JAMES ST BO 37 =

SPIKE MILLIGAN

BIRTHDAYS COME AND BIRTHDAYS GO

WE'RE GOVERNED BY LIFE'S EBB AND FLO

BUT AS I FACE THE NACKERS YARDS

I THANK YOU FOR YOUR KIND REGARDS =

LOVE NED THE DISAPPEARING TENOR +

CPD MN 930 4124

Teaching Alan Clare how to play the piano!!!

And finally – a sample of one of the hundred of letters Spike receives from children

Read - its
super

Dear Spike Mcllegan
    I think your poems are
Marvallos. I have Lots of poem
book's Myself. But out of all my
Poem Books my favrout one is
yours.
    Just a few days ago I Went
to See you in Theasure Illland
and I really thought jou were
the best.

I know all your Silly Verse
for Kids off by heart: poems
are my hobby and I try to coppy
your stile.

I am 9 years old and would
be thrild to have your autogrfe
and I will right one of the
poems I myself made up.
I Love I
Georgina

The Knot

The Knot has got a great big spot
Upon his tangled body
It is to me, as you may, See a dot from
uncle Noddy.
The dot, said the Knot, is planning a
a Plot he wants to untangle my body
If I Let him do this he'll get a big
Kiss from the daughter of P.C. Bobby.

The knot was unhappy as he said
to himself
Now how can I stop him all by myslef?
Then a rubber came running "Now how do you
do?
Shall I rub out that horibal spot for you"
"Well go right ahead" the happy knot
said.
And after all that the knot went
        to bed. by Georgina

Dear Georgina,

I think your letter is marvellous and I thought your poetry was very, very funny.

> There was a young girl called Georgina,
> And someone said 'Aye have you seen her?'
> Her mother said 'No'
> Ying Tong Diddle-I-Po
> She is upstairs drinking Ribena.

Love, Light and Peace,

SPIKE MILLIGAN

Afterword